DON'T MESS UP
MY TEMPO

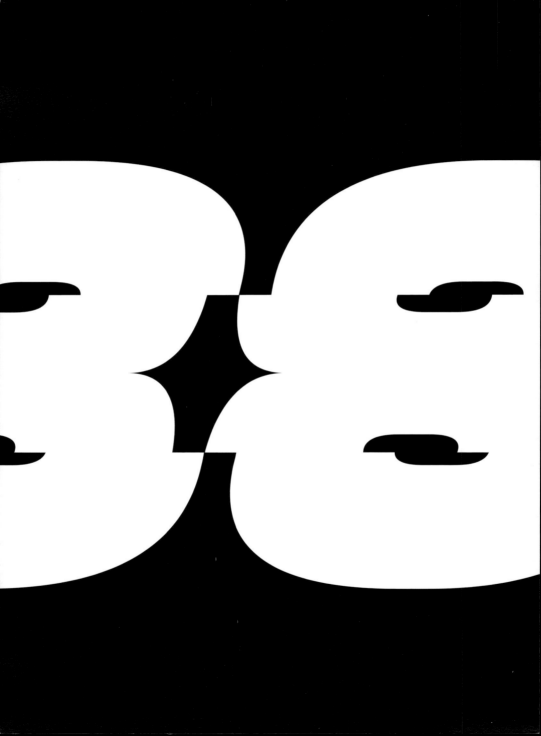

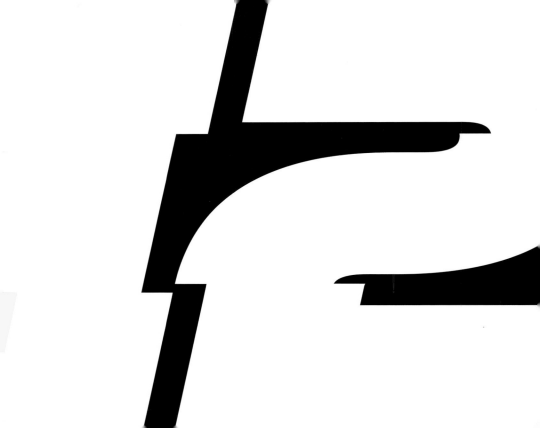

TRACK LIST

TEMPO

Korean Lyrics by JQ, 페노메코, 유영진
Composed by Jamil "Digi" Chammas, Leven Kali, Tay Jasper, Adrian McKinnon, MZMC
Arranged by Jamil "Digi" Chammas

* I can't believe 기다렸던 이런 느낌 나만 듣고 싶은 그녀는 나의 멜로디 하루 종일 go on and on and oh 떠나지 않게 그녈 내 곁에 ** Don't mess up my tempo 들어봐 이건 충분히 I said don't mess up my tempo 그녀의 맘을 훔칠 beat 어디에도 없을 리듬에 맞춰 1, 2, 3 Don't mess up my tempo 멈출 수 없는 이끌림 매혹적인 넌 lovely 틈 없이 좁혀진 거리 불규칙해지는 heartbeat 잠시 눈을 감아 trust me 밖으로 나갈 채비 미리 해둬 Are you ready? 오늘은 내가 캐리 도시 나 사이의 케미 이미 나와 농곤 뭐가 창피해 maboo 어정쩡 어버버 할 필요 없다고 챙길 건 없으니 손잡아 my lady 가는 길마다 레드 카펫 또 런웨이인걸 발걸음이 남달라 지금 이 속도 맞춰보자 tempo Baby girl 아침을 설레게 하는 모닝콜 매일 봐도 보고 싶은 맘인걸 지금부터 나와 Let's get down 모든 것이 완벽하게 좋아 So don't slow it up for me ** REPEAT 주월 둘러봐 lovely 틈 없이 좁혀진 거리 너에게 맞춰진 heartbeat 하고 싶은 대로 teach me 여긴 내 구역 Don't test me 혼자 있기 어색하다면 보내줘 message Now you got me flexin' 주월 둘러봐 널 보는 들러리 틈 속 위대한 개츠비 (Hold on wow) I'm doing alright baby girl you don't know 치윌 네 머리 위에 물음표 내 사전엔 없는 L.I.E 너는 이미 자연스럽게 맞추고 있어 내 tempo Baby girl 내 어깨에 살짝 기댄 그대의 아련한 향기가 다시 내 맘에 소용돌이치며 몰아친다 이대로 난 영원하고 싶다 So don't mess up my tempo baby Don't slow it up for me Don't mess up my tempo X7 내 눈을 바라보고 말해 나의 귓가에만 닿게 나만 사랑한다 말해 나밖에 없다고 말해 더 이상 흔들리지 않게 절대 널 뺏기지 않게 누구도 건들 수 없게 내 곁에 너를 지킬게 내 마음이 느껴지니 나를 감싸 안은 유일한 나만의 savior 모두 그런 널 바라보게 돼 * REPEAT Don't mess up my tempo 따라와 이건 충분히 I said don't mess up my tempo 완전히 다른 색의 beat 어디에도 없을 이런 완벽한 1, 2, 3 Don't mess up my tempo 멈출 수 없는 이끌림

Vocal Directed by DEEZ, Onestar
Background Vocals by EXO, Andrew Choi
Recorded by 정은경 @ In Grid Studio
　　　　　곽정신, 홍은이 @ The Vibe Studio
Digital Editing by 장우영 @ doobdoob Studio
Engineered for Mix by 이민규 @ SM Big Shot Studio
Mixed by 정의석 @ SM Blue Cup Studio

Original Title Tempo
Original Writers Jamil "Digi" Chammas, Leven Kali, Tay Jasper (Jeremy D Jasper), Adrian McKinnon, MZMC
Original Publishers Jamil Chammas Publishing, Orange Factory Music, Cuts of Reach Music, Palm Studios, AMM 7, WB Music Corp, Jeremy Jasper ASCAP Pub Designee, MARZ Music Group, LLC
Sub-Publishers Fujipacific Music Korea Inc., Warner/Chappell Korea Inc., EKKO Music Rights (powered by CTGA)

Production Administered by
MARZ Music Group, LLC & MZMC Publishing

SIGN

Korean Lyrics by JQ, Mola, 박유림 (makeumine works)
Composed by Harvey Mason Jr., Kevin Randolph, Patrick "J.Que" Smith, Dewain Whitmore, Britt Burton, Andrew Hey
Arranged by Harvey Mason Jr., Kevin Randolph

갈수록 희미해져 날 사랑했던 네 표정 감춰도 선명해져 조금씩 변해가는 너 너의 진심을 듣길 바래 now now now 뭘 그렇게 자꾸 말을 돌려 round round round Yeah 아닌 척 바라봐도 이미 이미 내게는 다 보이는 걸 모래처럼 넌 세게 쥘수록 내게서 흘어져 * 엇갈린 눈빛 걷잡을 수도 없이 번진 의심 비밀을 감춘 듯한 너의 sign sign sign 이제 그만 Don't lie lie lie 다 태워버릴 불꽃이 피어날지 몰라 네가 내게 던진 그 말 I know 그 모든 건 sign sign sign ** Honestly you da true X2 Body talk when you move X2 적막에 잠긴 공기 얼음 위를 걷듯 불안해 끝없는 이 악몽을 멈춰줘 더 늦기 전에 내가 기다리는 그 대답을 너는 이미 알고 있는데 적당히 넘어갈 생각은 마 차라리 나를 밀어내 실낱같았던 기대마저도 산산이 부서져 * REPEAT 결국 너는 갈라지게 돼 네가 뱉은 숱한 변명들의 밀실 안에 네가 놓은 덫에 혼자 계속해서 발이 걸려 Ringing a bell 머릿속에 like (ting!) 깨닫긴 넌 너무 늦었지 yah 너만 바랐던 마음 전부 한 줌의 재로 변해가 (날 돌이킬 수 없게 해) 흔적 없이 흩날린 네 기억들 모두 끝이라는 증거 점점 엇갈린 우리 걷잡을 수도 없이 번진 불길 하나 둘 드러나는 너의 sign sign sign 끝내 들킨 너의 lie lie lie 이별까지 모두 태워버릴지 몰라 날 사랑한다는 그 말 oh no 이쯤에서 bye bye bye ** REPEAT ** REPEAT

Vocal Directed by Onestar
Background Vocals by Onestar, Patrick "J. Que" Smith
Recorded by 우민정 @ In Grid Studio
Digital Editing by Ji-Young Shin NYC
Engineered for Mix by 이지홍 @ SM LVYIN Studio
Mixed by 김철순 @ SM Blue Ocean Studio

Original Title Body Don't Lie
Original Writers Harvey Mason Jr., Kevin Randolph, Patrick "J.Que" Smith, Dewain Whitmore, Britt Burton, Andrew Hey
Original Publishers Harvey Mason Music Publishing LLC, EKKO Music Rights (powered by CTGA), Hundredup East (Ascap) O/B/O Itself, Stankin Music (Ascap), Buddy & Bear Publishing (SESAC), Avex Music Publishing Inc., Seven Peaks Music, 8Sixteen Music, Hundredup East (Ascap) O/B/O Itself, Slangforhello (Ascap), Hundredup East (Ascap) O/B/O Britt Burton Songs (Ascap)
Sub-Publishers EKKO Music Rights (powered by CTGA), Universal Music Publishing Korea

OOH LA LA LA

닿은 순간

Korean Lyrics by 황유빈
Composed by Jamil "Digi" Chammas, Andrew Bazzi, Justin Lucas, Anthony Pavel, MZMC
Arranged by Jamil "Digi" Chammas, Justin Lucas

고개를 돌리면 눈이 마주치는 너 다시 한 번 또 빤히 날 쳐다보는 걸 그 미소는 좀 너무한 것 같아 애태우듯 여유가 넘쳐 숨이 막혀 배겨 없는 눈웃음에 아마 그게 매력인 걸 아는 듯해 yeah yeah yeah La la la la 너의 두 눈이 내게 속삭이는 건 La la la la 다가오라는 것 같아 * Ooh la la la 나를 허락해줘요 Ooh la la la 너의 상상 속으로 나 들어갈 테니 받아줘 그 눈 속에서 춤을 춰 Ooh la la la 시선이 닿은 순간 지금 이 순간 너와 나의 거리를 가득 채워버린 거센 이 떨림은 리듬이 되어 날 끌어당겨 끌리는 대로 넌 몸을 맡겨 Yeah she knows 알 듯 말 듯한 묘한 미소 나를 자극한 호기심도 꿰뚫은 채 보낸 신호 La la la la 살짝 열어둔 네 맘의 문을 열고 La la la la 들어오라는 것 같아 * REPEAT 이젠 진짜 움직여 가볼까 어떤 첫마디라면 좋을까 고민에 싸여 멈칫한 그 순간 네가 자릴 일어나서 걸어가 단호한 뒷모습은 보란 듯이 멀어져도 느린 발걸음은 오란 듯이 애매모호 Girl just tell me what you like, you like, you like, you like 서두르라는 것 같아 Ooh la la la 나를 허락해줘요 Ooh la la la 너의 현실 속으로 나 다가갈 테니 잡아줘 기다렸다고 말해줘 Ooh la la la 너에게 닿은 순간 Ah hoo 지금 네게 다가가 Ah hoo 가까워진 너와 나

Vocal Directed by G-high
Background Vocals by 변장문
Recorded by G-high @ MonoTree Studio
Digital Editing by G-high
　　　　장우영 @ doobdoob Studio
Engineered for Mix by 이민규 @ SM Big Shot Studio
Mixed by 남궁진 @ SM Concert Hall Studio

Original Title Ooh La La La
Original Writers Jamil "Digi" Chammas, Andrew Bazzi, Justin Lucas, Anthony Pavel, MZMC
Original Publishers Jamil Chammas Publishing, Orange Factory Music, Reach Music Publishing, Inc., EKKO Music Rights (powered by CTGA), Copyright Control, MARZ Music Group, LLC
Sub-Publishers Fujipacific Music Korea Inc., EKKO Music Rights (powered by CTGA)

GRAVITY

Korean Lyrics by 박찬열, 김민정
Composed by LDN Noise, DEEZ, Adrian McKinnon
Arranged by LDN Noise

Yeah woo uh woo uh nananana dadadada 영원히 날 사랑한다 그리 말하던 너야 내게 말했던 너야 그 말이 날 맴도는데 너를 어떻게 놓아 놓아 널 **baby** 아닌 걸 알지만 끝인 걸 알지만 자꾸만 난 (아직도 널 아직) 떠나려고 해도 꼭 같은 힘으로 난 널 붙잡고 있어 * 네 미래라 내게 그러더니 과거가 되었니 오직 나만 사랑한다더니 네 마음은 영원히 내 곁에만 머문다 그러더니 ** 내 전부를 걸었어 그랬더니 날 떠나버렸니 아직도 난 널 기다리잖니 내 마음은 여전히 널 끌어당겨 **gravity** 네 말투 문장 단어를 하나하나 기억 다 하는 나야 그날의 네가 날 맴도는데 너를 어떻게 놓아 놓아 널 **baby Believe**란 단어 속 숨겨져 있던 **lie** 그걸 못 봐 (아직도 난 아직) 너의 거짓말이 또 거짓일 거라고 날 속이고 있어 * **REPEAT** ** **REPEAT** 내가 걸었던 너란 배팅은 결국 **fail** 혼자서 독주하던 **raise Honey look at me now** 또 대답 없는 메아리만 돌아와 계속 맴돌기만 해 망가져가는 나를 또 뒤로한 채 네가 없는 이 우주를 떠돌까 두려워 널 위한다면 뭐든 움직일 힘이 있어 잘 알잖아 근데 네 마음만큼은 내 맘대로 안돼 아직 나를 끌어당기는 너의 무게는 계속 날 집어삼켜 갈수록 더 늘어가는 상처 이젠 추억도 자취를 감춰 머릿속에 번진 너의 모습들은 거짓 대체 뭘 믿어야 되는 건지 확신이 안 서 다시 또 너의 뒷모습에 소리쳐 (맴돌고 있어) * **REPEAT** 내 전부를 걸었어 그랬더니 날 떠나버렸니 아직도 난 널 기다리잖니 내 마음을 알잖니 난 널 믿었어 그랬더니

Directed by DEEZ
Background Vocals by CHEN, Andrew Choi, Adrian McKinnon
Recorded by 정은경, 우민정 @ In Grid Studio
Digital Editing by 장우영 @ doobdoob Studio
Engineered for Mix by 이지홍 @ SM LVYIN Studio
Mixed by

Original Title Gravity
Original Writers Greg Bonnick, Hayden Chapman, DEEZ, Adrian McKinnon
Original Publishers EKKO Music Rights (powered by CTGA), LDN Noise Pub Designee, Warner-Tamerlane Publishing Corp, WB Music Corp,

WITH YOU

가끔

Korean Lyrics by 박찬열, 김민지 (Jam Factory)
Composed by Sons Of Sonix, 박찬열
Arranged by Sons Of Sonix

환히 비춘 저 별들을 보면 너를 보는 것만 같지 반짝이는 모든 걸 닮은 너 밤하늘이 짙어져 가면 온 세상은 빛에 물들고 자연스레 내 손을 잡는 넌 어느새 내게 점점 물들어 * 그런 생각해 가끔 난 활짝 웃을 때 너를 보면 두 눈과 입꼬리 모두 다 나를 닮은 것 같아 보여 새까만 두 눈은 나란 빛을 머금어 나만이 환하게 빛나는 것 같아 가끔 난 너를 볼 때면 내가 보여 잠이 오지 않을 것 같은 오늘 밤이 난 이렇게나 좋을진 몰랐지 널 그릴 수 있는 시간이 유난히 yeah 우린 밤새 얘길 나누고 오늘 하루는 어땠었냐고 지금이 제일 좋다 하는 너 난 너로 인해 더 빛나는 걸 * REPEAT 매일매일 너를 바라보고 있는 나 나를 보고 있는 너 거울처럼 작은 표정부터 말투까지 다 내 모습이 느껴져 점점 하나가 돼가는 너와 나 너의 세상에 난 어떨까 하며 습관처럼 너의 눈동자 속 날 찾아 널 바라보다 깊어지는 밤 시간을 잠깐 멈추고서 난 내 눈에 담아두고 싶어 널 for me 그런 생각해 가끔 난 나와 꼭 닮은 너를 보면 사소한 것들도 모두 다 닮은 거였어 내가 널 지금 나에게 약속해 모든 빛이 사라질 때 꼭 오늘 밤처럼 언제나 나와 영원히 빛나줘 Love you

Vocal Directed by Onestar
Background Vocals by BAEKHYUN, CHANYEOL, SEHUN
Recorded by 김철순 @ SM Blue Ocean Studio
　　　　　이지홍 @ SM LVYIN Studio
　　　　　우민정 @ In Grid Studio
　　　　　민성수 @ doobdoob Studio
Digital Editing by 정호진 @ sound POOL studios
　　　Engineered for Mix by 이지홍 @ SM LVYIN Studio
Mixed by 이지홍 @ SM LVYIN Studio

Original Title F**k You
Original Writers Olaniyi Akinkunmi, Moses Samuels, Varren Wade, Aston Merrygold
Original Publishers Peermusic AB, Razor and Tie Music Publishing admin by peermusic, AIM Entertainments Limited by Kobalt Songs Music Publishing
Sub-Publisher Music Cube, Inc.

24/7

Korean Lyrics by Kenzie
Composed by Harvey Mason Jr., The Wavys, The Wildcardz, Aaron Berton, Andrew Hey
Arranged by The Wavys, The Wildcardz

Bye 그렇게 널 보내고 온 밤 역시 (밤 새 뒤척이네) 처음 내가 이상한 놈인지 생각해 왜 난 (낯선 기분인데) 수없이 혼자였던 날 익숙했던 그 공기 다 한순간에 훅 밀어내 들어와 내 작은방 차지한 노란 전구빛 같아 날 덥히던 너 * I think about it 24/7 '미안해' 보내도 전화는 오지 않네 I think about it 24/7 공허한 기분을 떨쳐낼 수 없네 기나 긴 하루 꿈꿔 next to you 네 생각뿐인 24/7 속은 타 미쳐가 조금씩 죽어가 넌 내 머릿속 박혀있고 네 맘엔 (얼음이 박혔지) 긴 날 동안 무슨 생각했을까 이젠 (내가 아플 시간) 왜 혼자여도 멀쩡한 아쉬울 게 없단 말 차갑다고 늘 잔소리 듣잖아 뭐가 그리 잘나서 yeah 좀 별로인 걸 아니깐 고치자 생각히 단순히 네게 잘 못하는 것뿐인데 난 차가운 게 아냐 그냥 많이 나빴어 * REPEAT 뻔해 보인 love movie scene 왜 그런 것들도 웃어쳤니 처음과 달리 변해버린 내 모습 오래도 참아쳤지 난 아무것도 없어 눈물 이제야 흘러 하루도 아니 한 시간도 못 견디게 보고픈데 * REPEAT 24/7

Vocal Directed by Kenzie
Background Vocals by CHEN
Recorded by 김철순 @ SM Blue Ocean Studio
이지홍 @ SM LVYIN Studio
우민정 @ In Grid Studio
Digital Editing by Ji-Young Shin NYC
Engineered for Mix by 이지홍 @ SM LVYIN Studio
Mixed by 남궁진 @ SM Concert Hall Studio

Original Title 24/7
Original Writers Harvey Jay Mason, Jack Brady, Jordan Roman, Ester Na, Sadie Currey, Aaron Berton, Andrew Hey
Original Publishers Harvey Mason Music Publishing LLC, EKKO Music Rights (powered by CTGA), Hundredup West (BMI), Hundredup East (Ascap) O/B/O Itself
Sub-Publisher EKKO Music Rights (powered by CTGA)

BAD DREAM

후폭풍

Korean Lyrics by 서지음
Composed by Mike Daley, Mitchell Owens, Bianca "Blush" Atterberry, DEEZ
Arranged by Mike Daley, Mitchell Owens

불안한 정적 넌 그 위로 덮쳐 넌 어느 틈에 또 어느 틈에 청해봐도 잠은 점점 달아나고 있어 좋은 모든 기억은 후회라는 색에 물들어 oh no no no 네가 없다는 사실이 난 안 믿겨 유난히도 큰 시계 소리 (tic toc tic toc) 불을 끈 뒤 눈을 감고 누우면 어디선가 잔잔하게 불어와 Woo 이건 너인 것 같아 네가 흩날리기 시작해 Woo 텅 빈 바람 소린 점점 폭풍이 되어 * 이상할 만큼 고요했던 내게로 삼킬 듯이 다가오는 나쁜 꿈 난 마비된 채 움직일 수 없어 휘몰아친 네 안에 잠겨 ** 모든 감정이 (한꺼번에) 너와의 이별이 (한꺼번에) 다 지금 여기 한꺼번에 덮쳐 난 난 난 휘몰아친 네 안에 있어 마지못해 안녕 그게 최선이었다고 단정 지어버렸던 그때의 날 누가 말려줘 oh no no no 그건 진심이 아니었다 말해도 너의 맘은 다 닫혔겠지 돌아갈 수 없는 틈을 스치고 나를 베어버린 날 카로운 숨 Woo 이건 너인 것 같아 네가 아파오기 시작해 Woo 이제서야 끝이 난 게 실감이 났어 * REPEAT ** REPEAT 너를 놓지 못해 이제 와서야 뒤늦게 이런 날 부디 알아도 모른척해 아직 어제 같아 여전히 시간이 지나도 넌 이렇게 그려져 번져 이상할 만큼 고요했던 내게로 (내게 점점 더) 삼킬 듯이 다가오는 나쁜 꿈 (삼킬 듯이 와) 난 마비된 채 움직일 수 없어 휘몰아친 네 안에 잠겨 (네게 잠겨) ** REPEAT 잘 지내라고 했는데 잊어달라고 했는데 나도 그러고 싶은데 그게 맘대로 잘 안돼 온 힘을 다해 버릴게 모든 바람이 걷힐 때 그땐 너처럼 웃을게

Directed by DEEZ
Background Vocals by Andrew Choi
Recorded by 이민규 @ SM Big Shot Studio
　　　　　　이지홍 @ SM LVYIN Studio
　　　　　　장우영 @ doobdoob Studio
　　　　　　정은경 @ In Grid Studio
　　　　　　곽정신, 정모연 @ The Vibe Studio
Digital Editing by 장우영 @ doobdoob Studio
Engineered for Mix by 이지홍 @ SM LVYIN Studio
Mixed by 김철순 @ SM Blue Ocean Studio

Original Title Stranger
Original Writers Mike Daley, Mitchell Owens, Bianca "Blush" Atterberry, DEEZ
Original Publishers 7210 Publishing, LLC (ASCAP), EKKO Music Rights (powered by CTGA), Seven Summits Music (BMI) Life Publishing o/b/o Itself and High Rise
Sub-Publisher EKKO Music Rights (powered by CTGA)

DAMAGE

Korean Lyrics by 신진혜 (Jam Factory)
Composed by LDN Noise, DEEZ, Adrian McKinnon
Arranged by LDN Noise

Damage (damage) Damage (damage) Damage 넌 무덤덤한 얼굴로 거짓을 또 내뱉어 다 알면서 난 마치 습관처럼 흔들려 숨이 안 쉬어져 추억에 젖어 더 깊어지는 방황 앞에 내 믿음이 무너져 한 번의 거짓말이 날은 거짓 어디까지 너였나 한숨만 계속 붙어내고 있어 눈앞이 흐려져가 어두워진 밤에 모르게 나를 따돌리던 게 악몽이라고 치부하기엔 불안이 끝도 없던 밤 암흑 속에 넌 끝내 날 깨워 봐 버려봐도 다 너 때문에 * (You) 다치고 또 다치게 해 다 너 때문에 (You) 커진 damage 네가 담겨 놓은 내 신호탄 (모든 순간) 되돌리기엔 너무 커진 damage ** (You) 얽히고 또 덮친 어둠 다 너 때문에 (You) 생긴 damage 야차 싫은 그 순간 (알겠지만) 난 이미 멀리 떠나 Da-damage Damage Damage Damage Damage 닥쳐올 거야 후회가 내 바닥난 인내를 봐 말라버린 기대와 내 의무감도 끌고 갈수록 또 깊어진 상처 떠난 후에 넌 느껴 답해봐 너도 uh 희미하게 비친 웃음에 감춰진 너의 진심 이젠 내 맘이 no no 불안한 어둠이 쓰라린 기억이 몰아치는 이 밤 혼란 속에 넌 끝내 날 깨워 봐 참아봐도 다 너 때문에 * REPEAT ** REPEAT 다 끝난 일인 걸 돌아갈 수 없음을 no no no 다른 누군가를 만나 사랑할 수만 있다면 yeah 생각하면 생각할수록 내 맘의 상처는 더 깊어져 and I know 내게는 또 다른 사랑은 없어 EXO 다 너 때문에 * REPEAT (You) 겹치고 또 겹친 어둠 다 너 때문에 (You) 생긴 damage 결국 나였다는 걸 (알겠지만) 난 이미 멀리 떠나 Da-damage Damage Damage Damage Damage X2 멀리 떠나 멀리 떠나 Da-damage

Directed by DEEZ
Background Vocals by Andrew Choi, Adrian McKinnon
Recorded by 정은경, 우민정 @ In Grid Studio
　　　　　　 김광민 @ 개나리싸운드
　　　　　　 민성수 @ doobdoob Studio
Digital Editing by 정호진 @ sound POOL studios
Engineered for Mix by 이민규 @ SM Big Shot Studio
Mixed by 이민규 @ SM Big Shot Studio

Original Title Damage
Original Writers Greg Bonnick, Hayden Chapman, DEEZ, Adrian McKinnon
Original Publishers EKKO Music Rights (powered by CTGA), LDN Noise
Pub Designee, Warner-Tamerlane Publishing Corp, WB Music Corp, AMM7
Sub-Publishers EKKO Music Rights (powered by CTGA), Warner/Chappell
Music Korea Inc.

Track Produced by LDN Noise

SMILE ON MY FACE

여기 있을게

Korean Lyrics by JQ, 박지희 (makeumine works)
Composed by Brian Kennedy, Iain James, Samuel Jensen
Arranged by Brian Kennedy

어렴풋한 기억에 그마저도 이젠 꽤 희미해 이름조차 잘 떠오르지 않아 그날은 너무 또렷한데 어쩌면 넌 heartbreaker 내 맘을 아프게 했던 게 분명한데 이렇게 아무렇지 않은 날 보면 이젠 다 괜찮은가봐 그랬던 널 우연히 마주친 거야 하얗게 잊혀진 너는 또 그렇게 스쳐 지나가는 바람처럼 넌 사라져가 자연스레 * I did it all with a smile on my face 내 기억에 사라진 흔적들이 나에게 다시 돌아올까봐 웃으며 다시 돌려보낼게 I did it all with a smile on my face 아무도 아파하지 않아도 돼 멀어져가는 널 붙잡지 않아 난 웃으며 널 떠나보내 With a smile on my face 한참을 멍하니 서서 저만치 멀어져간 널 바라보네 왜 이러는지 나도 이해가 안 돼 널 보냈던 그날처럼 물었어 이유가 뭐냐 아무 말 없이 날 꼭 안아줬고 그게 우리의 끝인 걸 알았어 그렇게 멀어져간 너 사실 너에 대한 모든 건 선명해 네 이름 눈빛 말투까지 모든 게 사랑했던 기억 마음 깊숙이 묻어둘래 자연스레 * REPEAT 원한다면 나 있을게 있을게 여기 이대로 나 있을게 내가 있을게

Vocal Directed by 서미래 (ButterFly)
Background Vocals by CHEN, 서미래 (ButterFly)
Recorded by 이민규 @ SM Big Shot Studio
장우영 @ doobdoob Studio
G-high @ Monotree Studio
김광민 @ 게나리싸운드
Pro Tools Operaiting by 서미래 (ButterFly)
Digital Editing by 서미래 (ButterFly)
Engineered for Mix by 이지홍 @ SM LVYIN Studio
Mixed by 남궁진 @ SM Concert Hall Studio

Original Title Smile On My Face
Original Writers Brian Kennedy, Iain James, Samuel Jensen
Original Publishers Kennedy Klassiks Music (ASCAP) Administered by Kobalt Songs Music Publishing (ASCAP), Kobalt Music Services Limited (BMI) Administered by Songs of Kobalt Music Publishing (BMI), EMI April Music Inc., Normaharris Music Publishing, Sam Hook Music, Strauss Co LLC
Sub-Publishers Music Cube, Inc., EMI Music Publishing Korea

OASIS

오아시스

Korean Lyrics by 조윤경
Composed by Kevin White, Mike Woods, Andrew Bazzi, MZMC
Arranged by Rice n' Peas

화려했던 모든 게 날 유혹하듯 이어진 그곳만이 세상의 전부인 줄만 알았어 거칠어진 숨 해답을 찾기 바쁜 눈 말라가는 내 입술 끝없이 이어진 이 길 우린 * 조금 더 멀리 더 멀리 아득한 이 길을 따라 Runnin' I'm runnin' Chasing the sun 긴 하루를 Run Run Run Run 만들어진 길엔 결국 모두 끝이 있다는 걸 알아버린 내게 문득 답을 되묻듯 네 멋대로 가 굳이 멈추지는 마 방향 따원 재지마 헤맬수록 목이 타 yeah yeah 붉게 물든 desert 너머 오아시스 찾아 나서 * REPEAT ** 우린 더 멀리 더 멀리 간 적 없는 길을 찾아 Runnin' I'm runnin' Chasing the sun Yeah I'm on the road 보다 먼 그곳을 더 나는 갈망하는 걸 타들어 갈 목마름에 난 oh * REPEAT ** REPEAT Run Run Run Run Yeah I'm on the road

Vocal Directed by 주찬양 (ICONIC SOUNDS)
Background Vocals by 주찬양 (ICONIC SOUNDS)
Recorded by 정은경 @ In Grid Studio
　　　　　　곽정신, 홍은이 @ The Vibe Studio
Digital Editing by Ji-Young Shin NYC
Engineered for Mix by 이지름 @ SM LVYIN Studio
Mixed by 정의석 @ SM Blue Cup Studio

Original Title Runnin'
Original Writers Mike Woods, Kevin White, Andrew Bazzi, MZMC
Original Publishers EKKO Music Rights (powered by CTGA), MARZ Music Group, LLC
Sub-Publisher EKKO Music Rights (powered by CTGA)

Production Administered by
MARZ Music Group, LLC & MZMC Publishing

TEMPO

节奏

Chinese Lyrics by 深白色 *(Arys Chien)*
Composed by Jamil "Digi" Chammas, Leven Kali, Tay Jasper, Adrian McKinnon, MZMC
Arranged by Jamil "Digi" Chammas

*I can't believe 整个世界 为她着迷 无法不去在意 纠缠耳膜的 melody 反复回忆 go on and on and oh 跟随 这旋律 留住你痕迹 ** Don't mess up my tempo 接受它 用心去倾听 I said don't mess up my tempo 这 是我偷心的武器 别乱了我节奏 独一无二的 one two three Don't mess up my tempo 她是我专属 melody 和你一起 so lovely 窄窄的街道 有魔力 变得不规则的 heartbeat 闭上眼睛聆听 trust me 时间还没到 我就等在这 里 Are you ready? 来培养一点这都市和我之间的默契 Don't be shy nobody is ever ready yea ma boo 不需要 又想坏 又想乖 何必 Oh 牵着我 跟着我 I'll show you my lady 走到哪里都有玫瑰花瓣铺地 走路姿态像传奇 Girl we just ride now to the beat my tempo Baby girl 你的 morning call 让我世界开机 每天见面也 还是分秒想你 就从现在开始 Let's get down 一切美好得难以相信 So don't slow it up for me ** REPEAT 魅惑我的你 lovely 越阻挡就越是无力 再激烈都可以 OK 只要是你想要 teach me 在我的地盘 Don't test me 如果你落单感到不安就给我 message Now you got me flexin' 现在看清楚 我是这刺激的街道 伟大的盖茨比 (Hold on wow) I'm doing alright baby girl you don't know 脸上所有的问号都抛弃 我字典里没有 L.I.E 你还没注意 但你早已经踏入了我的 tempo Baby girl 当你微微靠着我的脸呼吸 那阵气息引起无尽的涟漪 像游涡般 突然向我袭击 希望时间就停在 right now So don't mess up my tempo baby Don't slow it up for me Don't mess up my tempo X7 请看着我的眼睛诉说 贴在我的耳边诉说 告诉我你只想爱我 告诉我你只拥有我 别 再听谁的道听途说 绝不让你被谁诱惑 对手出现绝不啰唆 守护着你的会是我 Can you feel it Feel my heartbeat 包围着我的你 专属的 唯一的 savior 全世界暂停 全在看着你 * REPEAT ** REPEAT

Vocal Directed by DEEZ, Onestar
Background Vocals by EXO, Andrew Choi
Recorded by Eun-Kyung Jeong @ In Grid Studio
　　　　　　　Jung-Shin Kwak, Eun-Yi Hong @ The Vibe Studio
Digital Editing by Woo-Young Jang @ doobdoob Studio
Engineered for Mix by Min-Kyu Lee @ SM Big Shot Studio
Mixed by Eui-Seok Jung @ SM Blue Cup Studio

Chinese Lyricist 深白色 *(Arys Chien)*
Original Publisher MO ER GUO JI YU LE GU FEN YOU XIAN GONG SI
Sub-Publishers Warner/Chappell Music Taiwan Ltd, Warner/Chappell
Music Korea Inc.

Original Title Tempo
Original Writers Jamil "Digi" Chammas, Leven Kali, Tay Jasper (Jeremy
D Jasper), Adrian McKinnon, MZMC
Original Publishers Jamil Chammas Publishing, Orange Factory Music,
Cuts of Reach Music, Palm Studios, AMM 7, WB Music Corp, Jeremy
Jasper ASCAP Pub Designee, MARZ Music Group, LLC
Sub-Publishers Fujipacific Music Korea Inc., Warner/Chappell Korea Inc.,
EKKO Music Rights (powered by CTGA)

Production Administered by
MARZ Music Group, LLC & MZMC Publishing

CREDITS

Executive Producer SM ENTERTAINMENT Co., Ltd.
Producer SOO-MAN LEE
Music & Sound Supervisor YOUNG-JIN YOO

Producing Director
Chris Lee
A&R Direction & Coordination
Jin-Hyun Lee, Gyu-Jae Jung, Kyung-Joo Kim, Ma Yin Ying
International A&R
Rachel S. Lee, Kay Kim, Jamie Lee, Emily Oh
Music Licensing
Jung-Eun Oh, Min-Joo Cha
Music Production Management
Hui-Mok Kang, A-Ruem Yu
Artist Planning & Development
Hee-Jun Yoon, Yu-Eun Cho, Pyung-Hwa Shin
Recorded by
Chul-Soon Kim @ SM Blue Ocean Studio
Min-Kyu Lee @ SM Big Shot Studio
Ji-Hong Lee @ SM LYVIN Studio
Eun-Kyung Jeong, Min-Jung Woo @ In Grid Studio
Woo-Young Jang, Seong-Su Min @ doobdoob Studio
Jung-Shin Kwak, Mo-Yeon Jung, Eun-Yi Hong @ The Vibe Studio
Kwang-Min Kim @ GaeNaRi Sound
G-high @ MonoTree Studio
Mixed by
Jin Namkoong @ SM Concert Hall Studio
Jong-Pil Gu (BeatBurger) @ SM Yellow Tail Studio
Chul-Soon Kim @ SM Blue Ocean Studio
Eui-Seok Jung @ SM Blue Cup Studio
Min-Kyu Lee @ SM Big Shot Studio
Ji-Hong Lee @ SM LYVIN Studio
Mastered by
Chris Gehringer @ Sterling Sound

Management Director
Young-Jun Tak
Artist Management & Promotion
Joo-Young Kim, Seung-Hwan Lee, Jin-Wook Bang, Yong-Min Noh,
Hee-Kyung Kang, Sung-Ho Park, Seung-Hwan Kim, Yun-Seok Park,
Seung-Hwan Yang
Public Relations & Publicity
Eun-A Kim, Sang-Hee Jung, Ji-Sun Lee, Seol-Hee Kang, Ji-Hyun Jeon
Media Planning
Min-Sung Kim, Min-Kwon Bok, Jae-Hyuk Huh, Ho-Sik Kim
Choreography Direction
Young-Jun Tak, Seong-Yong Hong
Choreographer
Rie Hata, Mihawk Back
International Marketing
Mina Jungmin Choi
Customer Relationship Management
Eun-A Kim, Yoon-Joo Tark, Jung-A Lee

Creative Director
Hee-Jin Min
Music Video Direction & Arrangement
Hee-Jin Min, Ye-Min Kim
Music Video Director
Daniel Jon
Graphic Design
Woo-Cheol Jo, Ye-Min Kim, Woo-Sik Jo
(Assistant. Han-Gyeol Kim, Sae-Rom Son)
Jacket Styling
Ji-Seok Park
Music Video Styling
Ji-Seok Park, Ah-Ran Lee
Hair Styling
Nae-Joo Park $^{EXO-K}$, Yoon-Jeong Choi $^{EXO-M}$
Make-Up
Yun-Su Hyun $^{EXO-K}$, Mi-Hye Jo $^{EXO-M}$
Photography
Si-Young Song

Management and Marketing Executive
SO-YOUNG NAM, SE-MIN HAN
Executive Supervisor
YOUNG-MIN KIM

Official Homepage
EXO Official Homepage
http://exo.smtown.com
EXO Official Global Fanclub 'EXO-L' Homepage
http://exo-l.smtown.com
SM ENTERTAINMENT Official Homepage
http://www.smtown.com

Social Network Service
EXO Facebook
https://www.facebook.com/weareoneEXO
EXO Twitter
https://twitter.com/weareoneexo
EXO Instagram
https://www.instagram.com/weareone.exo
EXO Weibo
https://weibo.com/weareoneexo

YouTube Channel
https://www.youtube.com/weareoneexo